Mediocre Photographs of Rocks

By L. Rogers

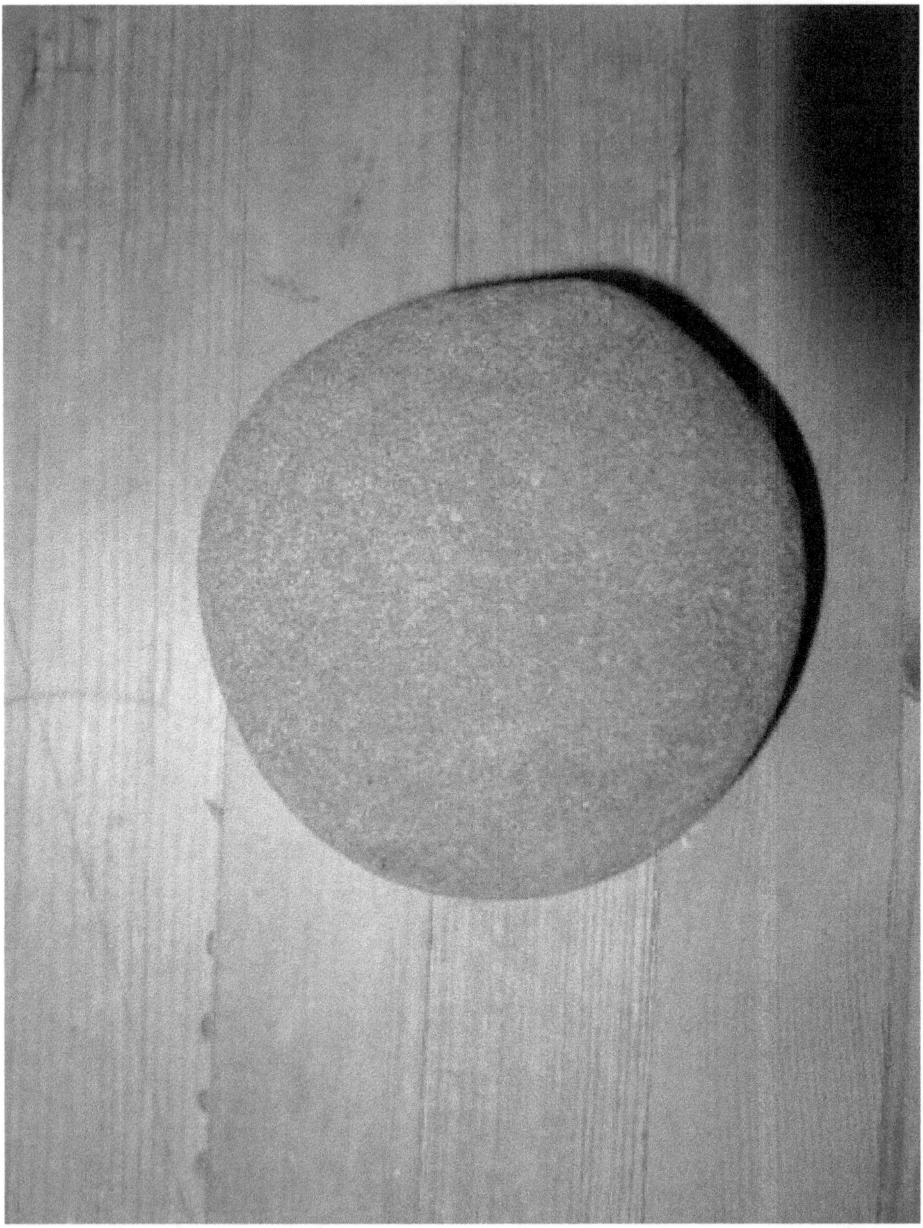

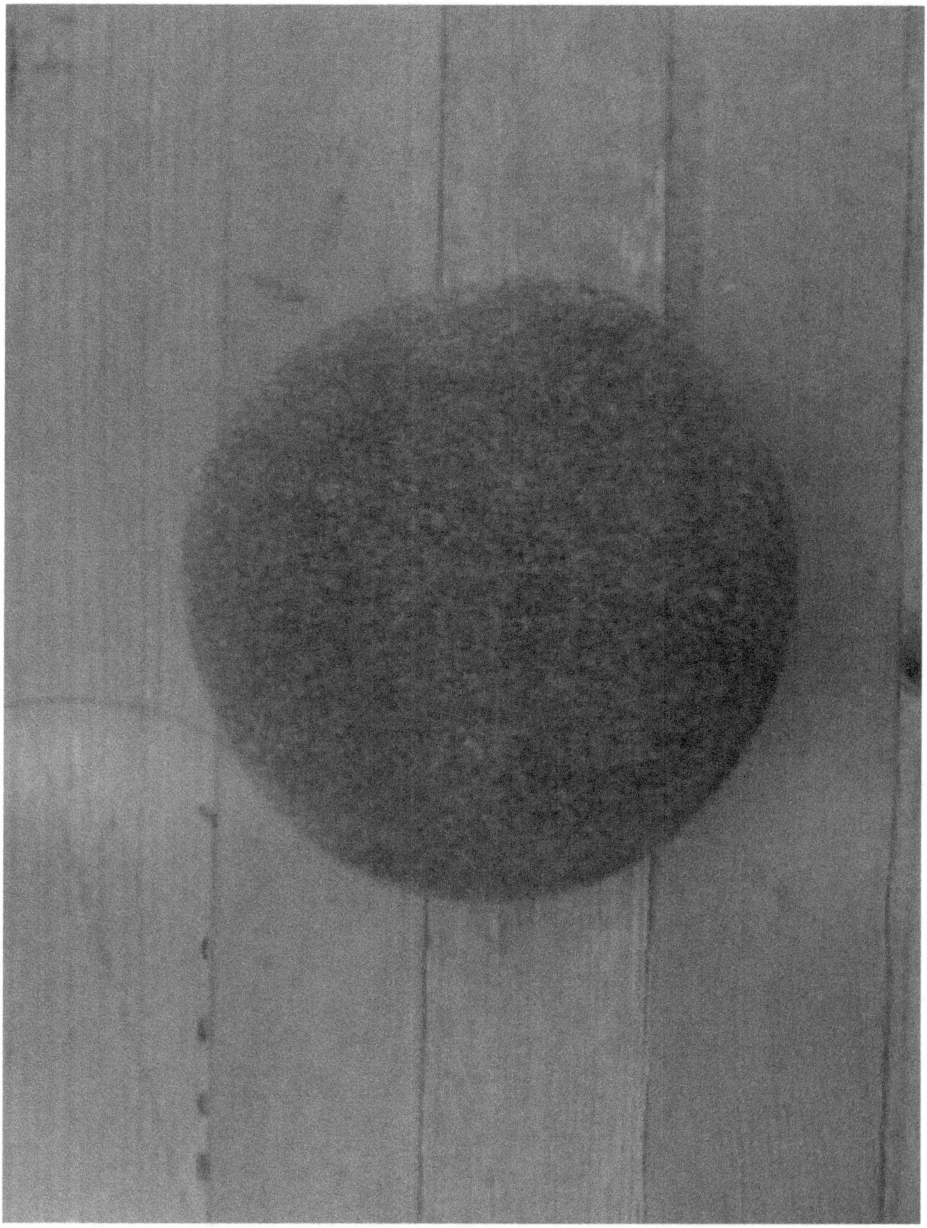

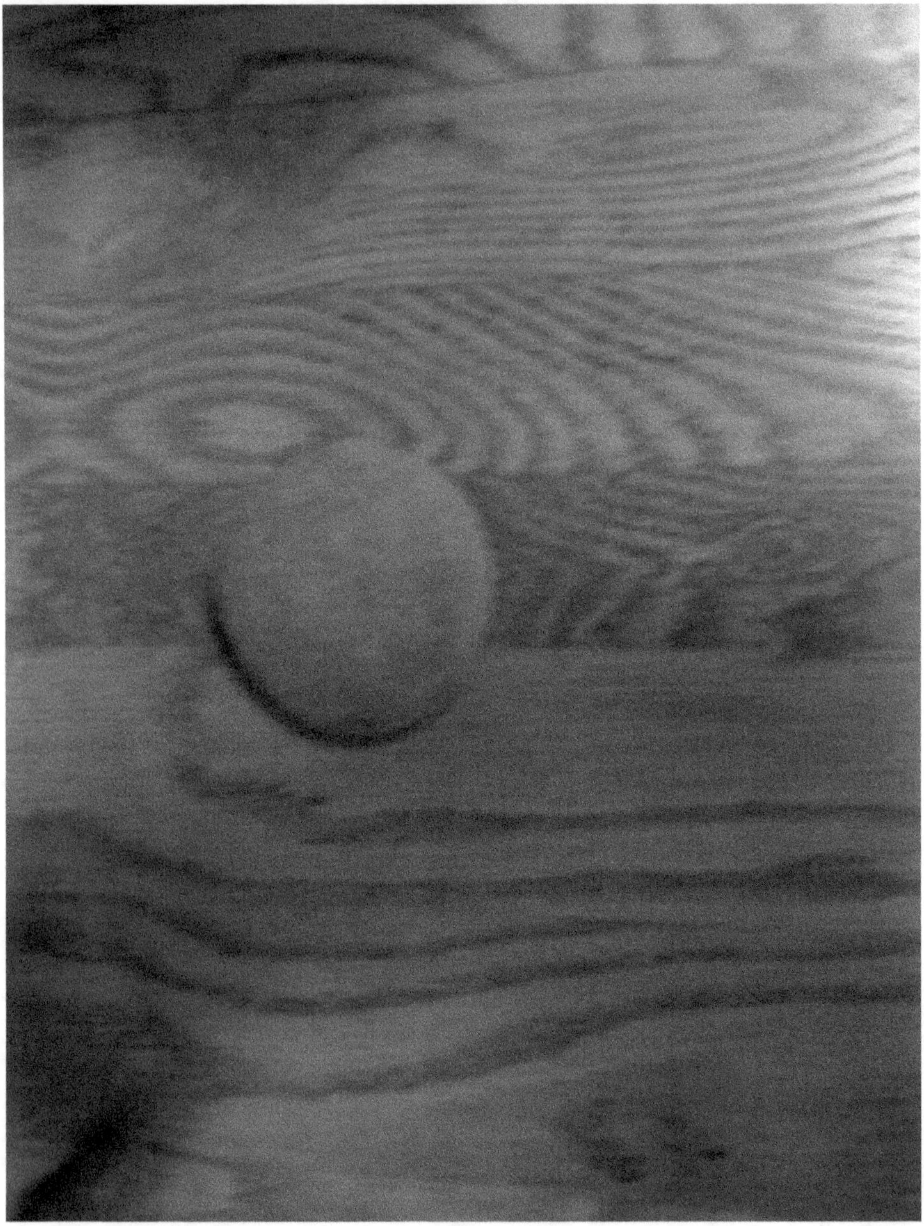

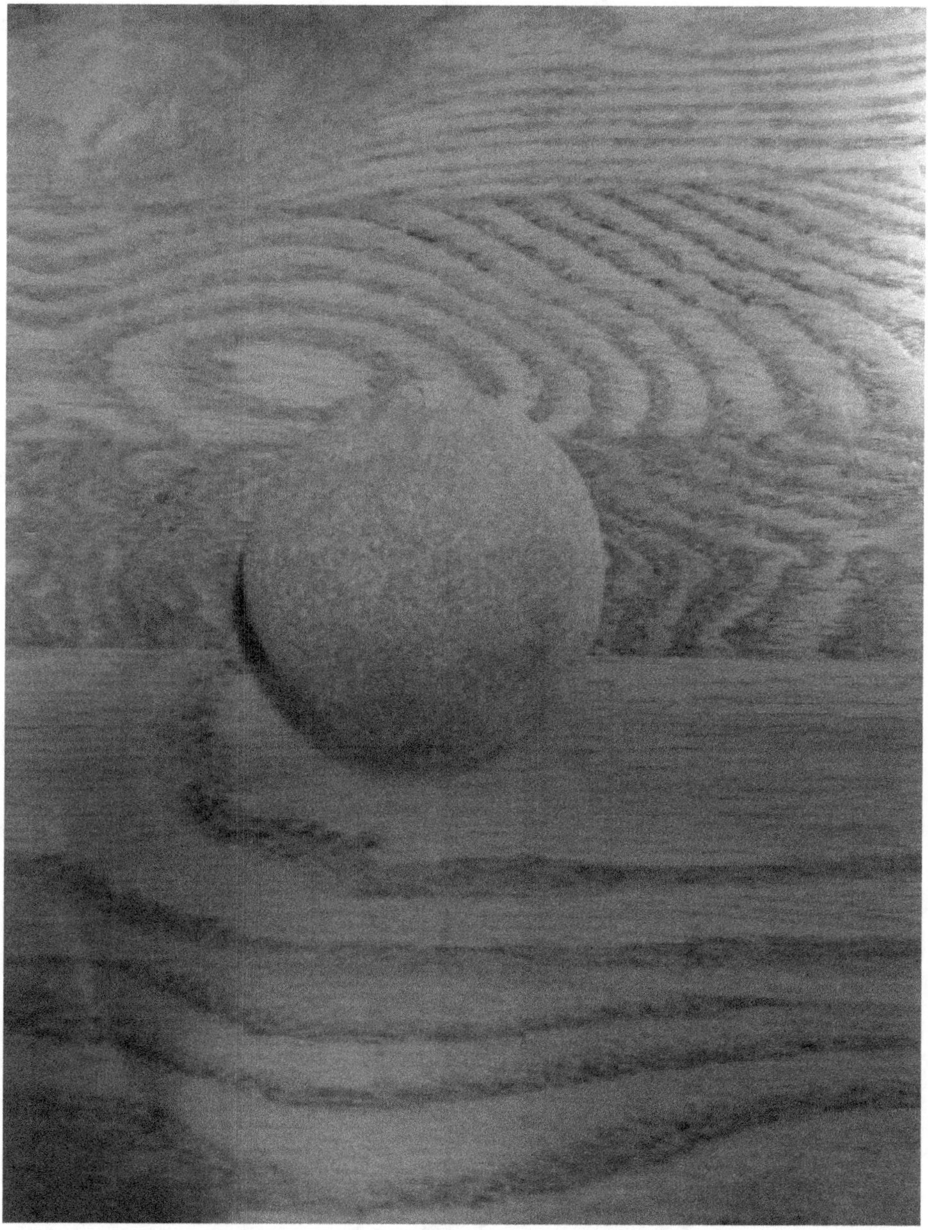

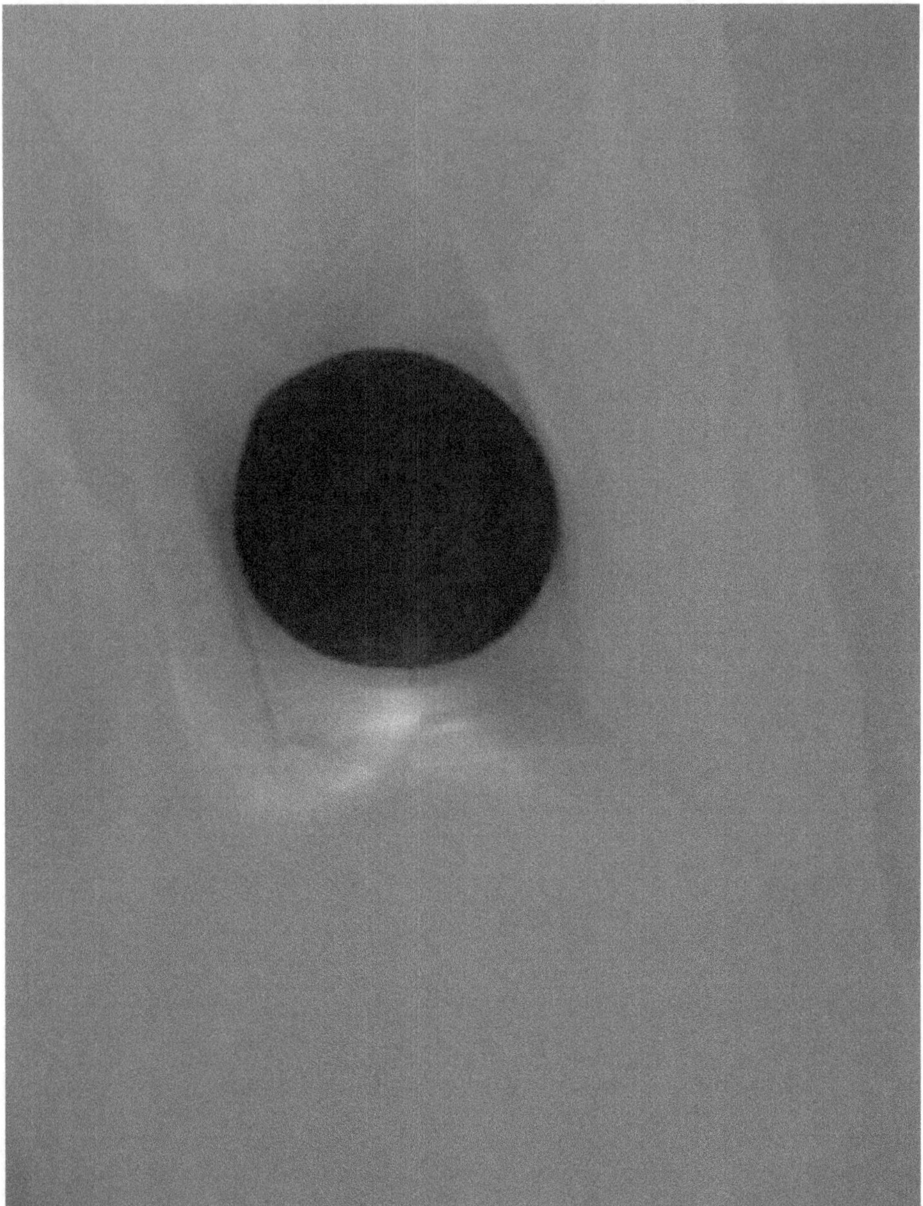

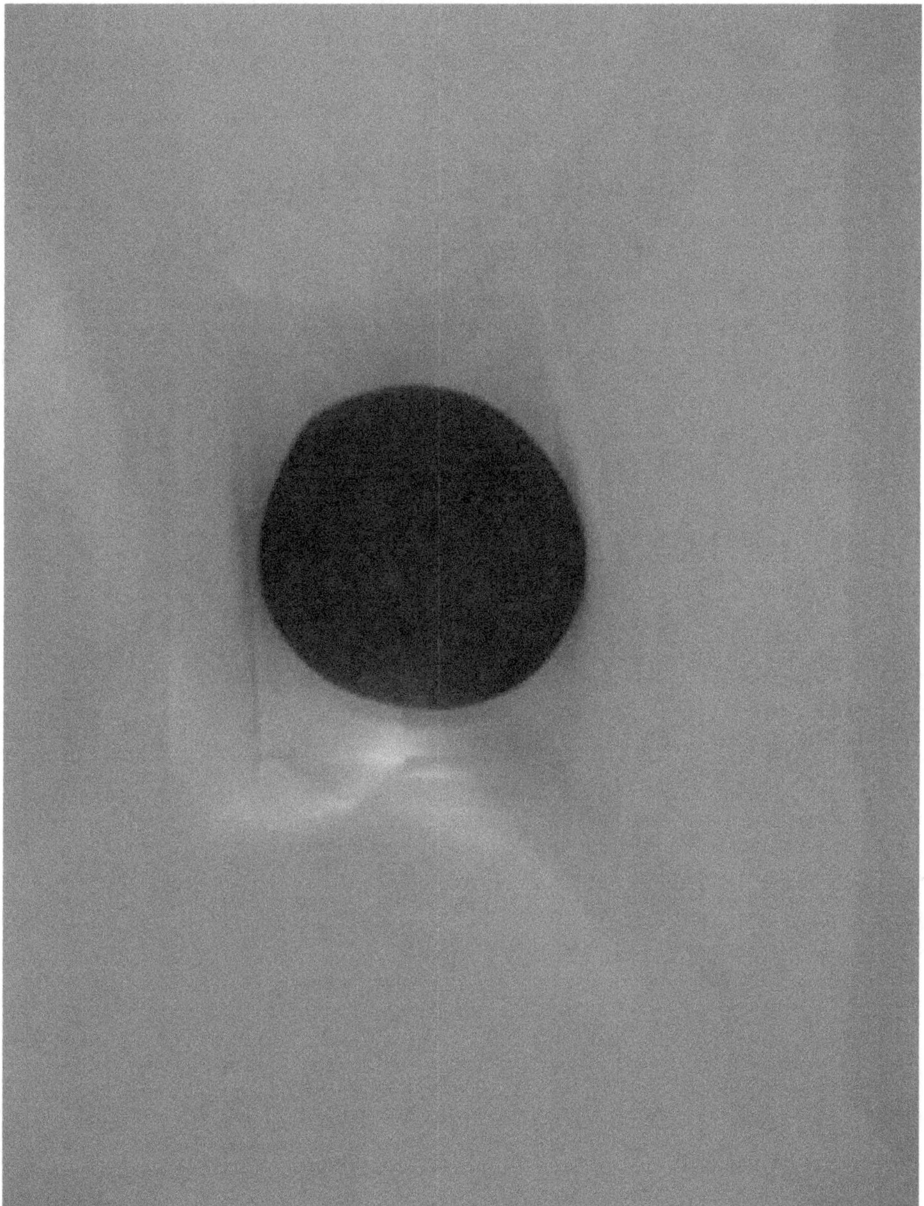

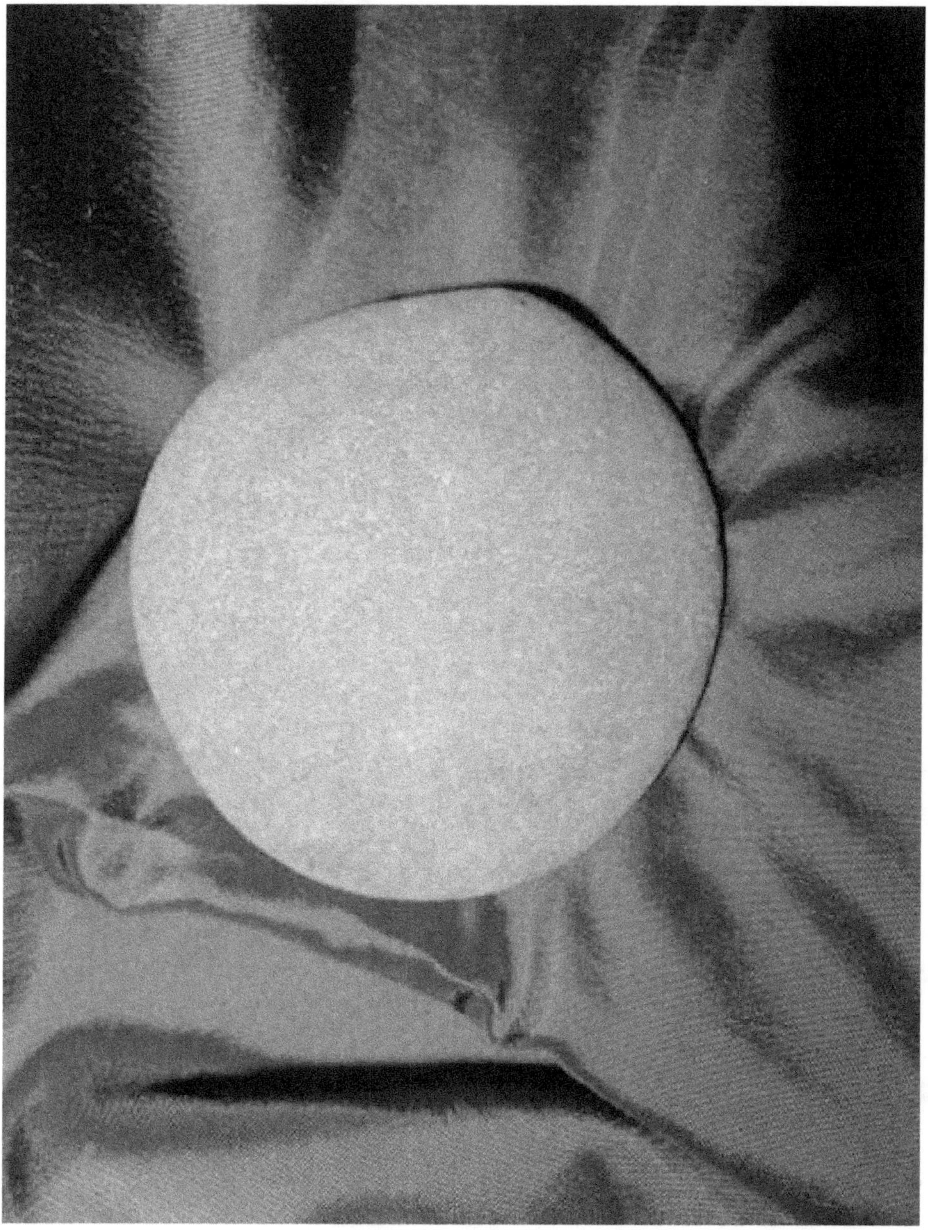

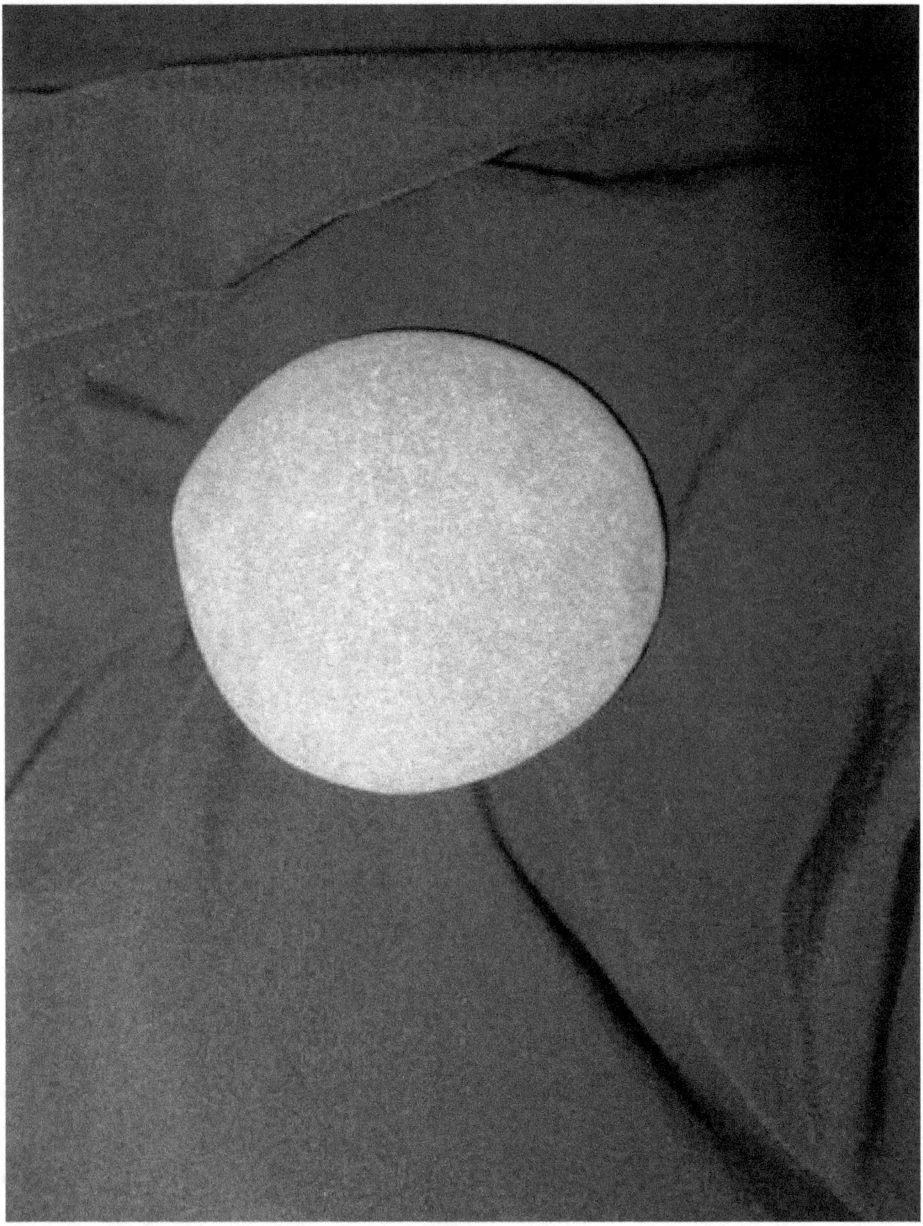

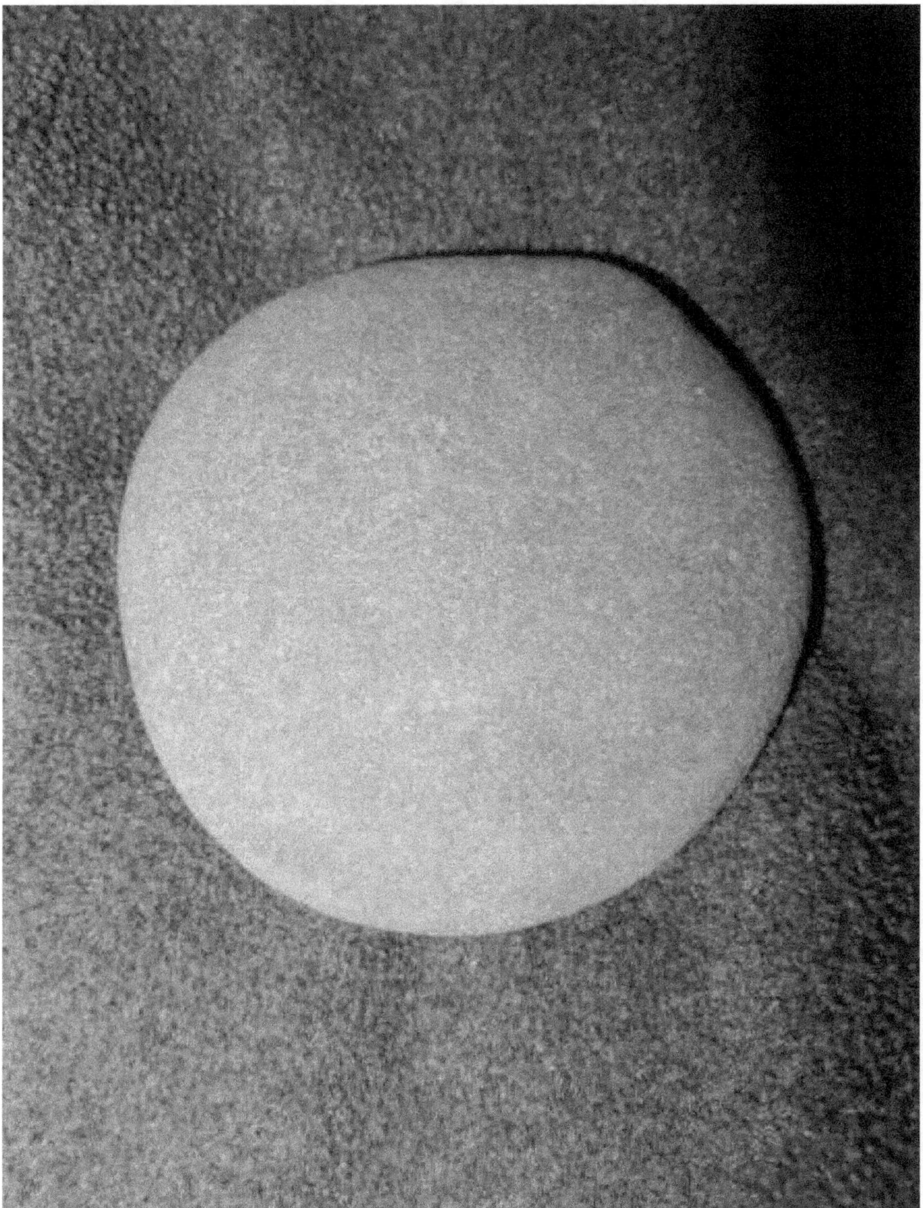

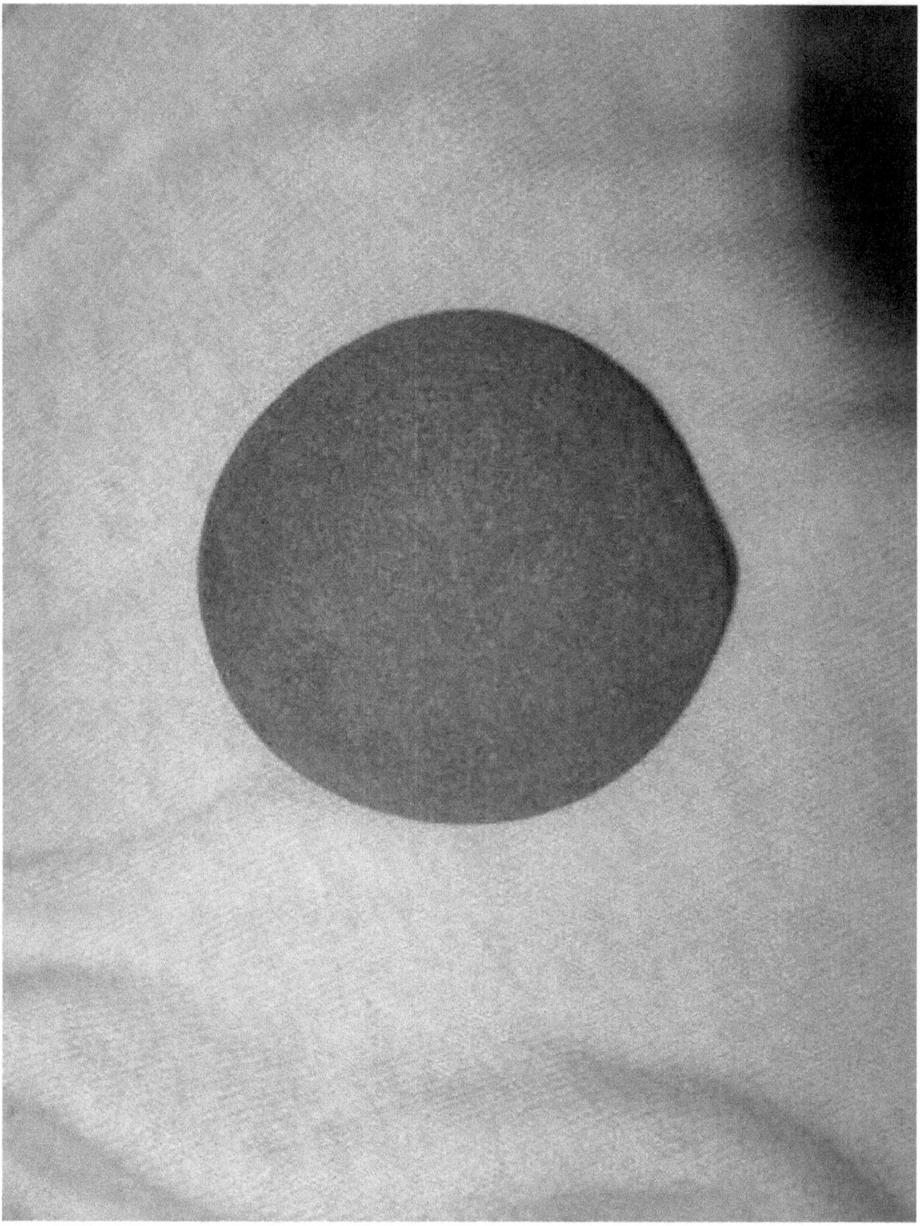

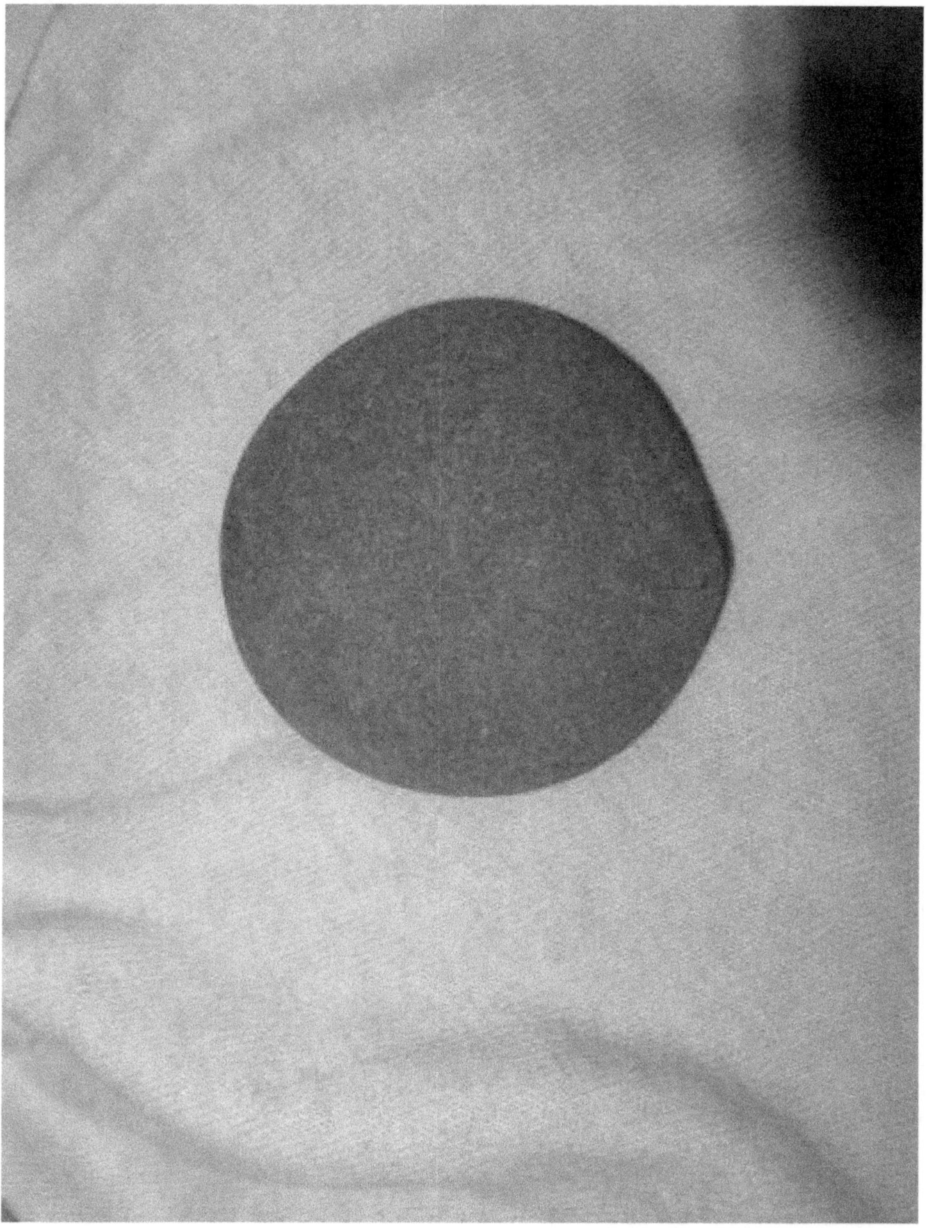

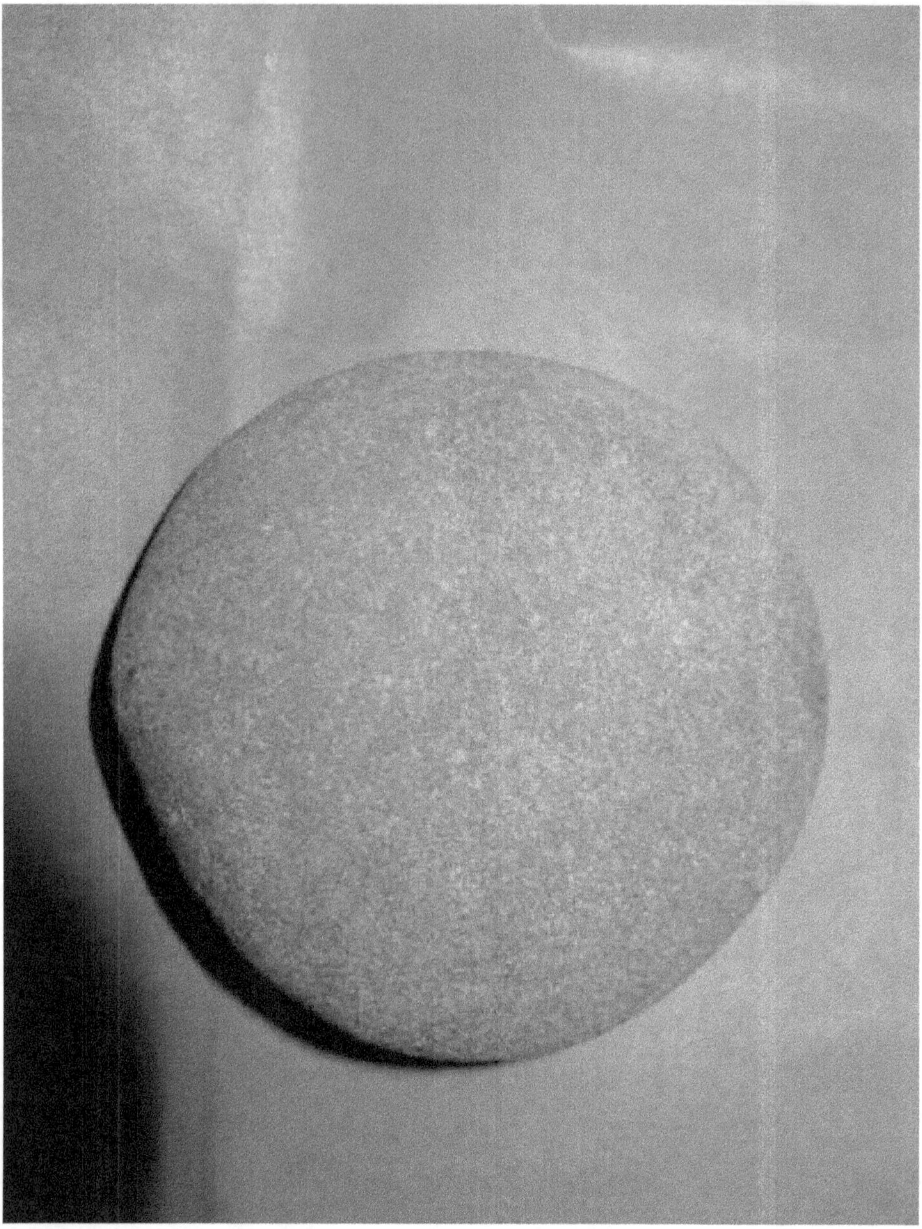

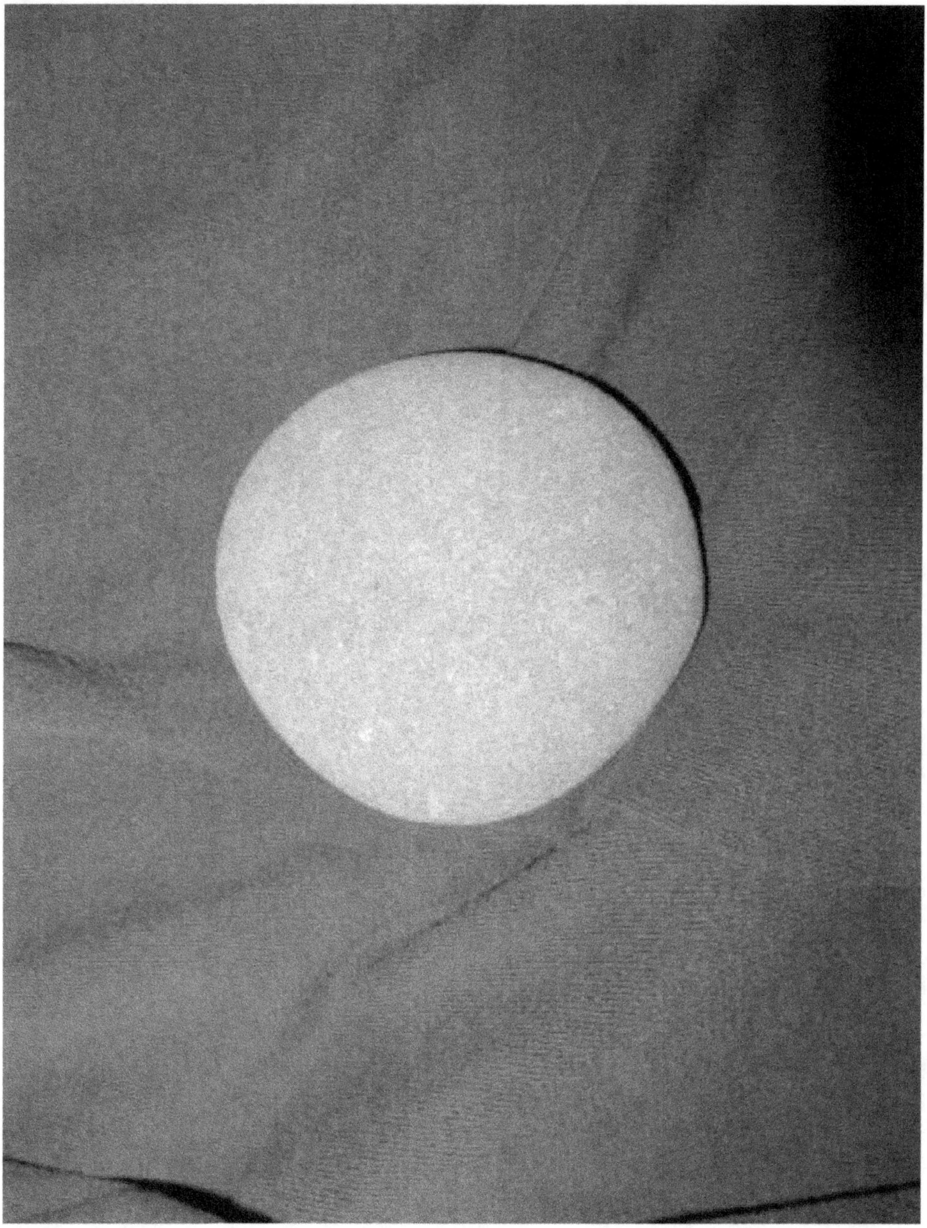

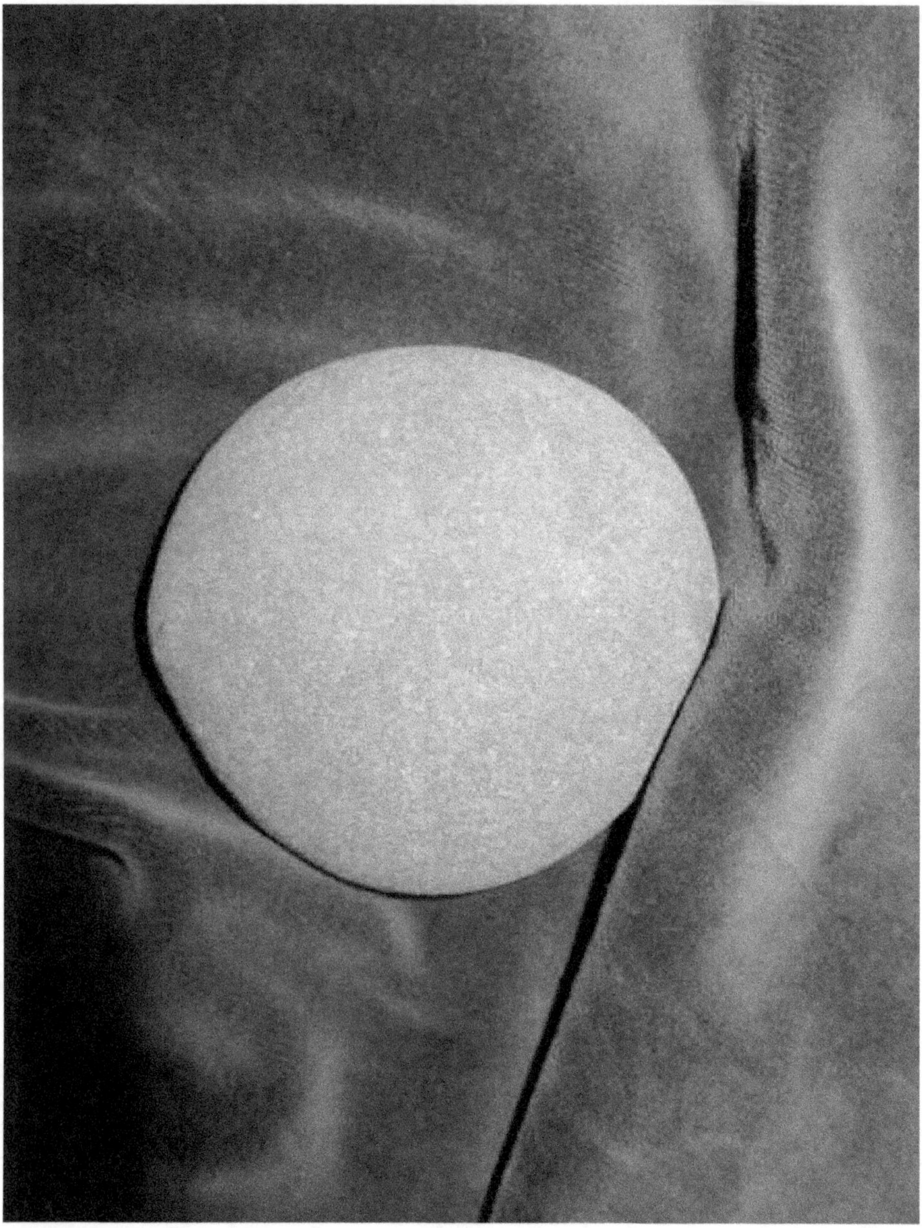

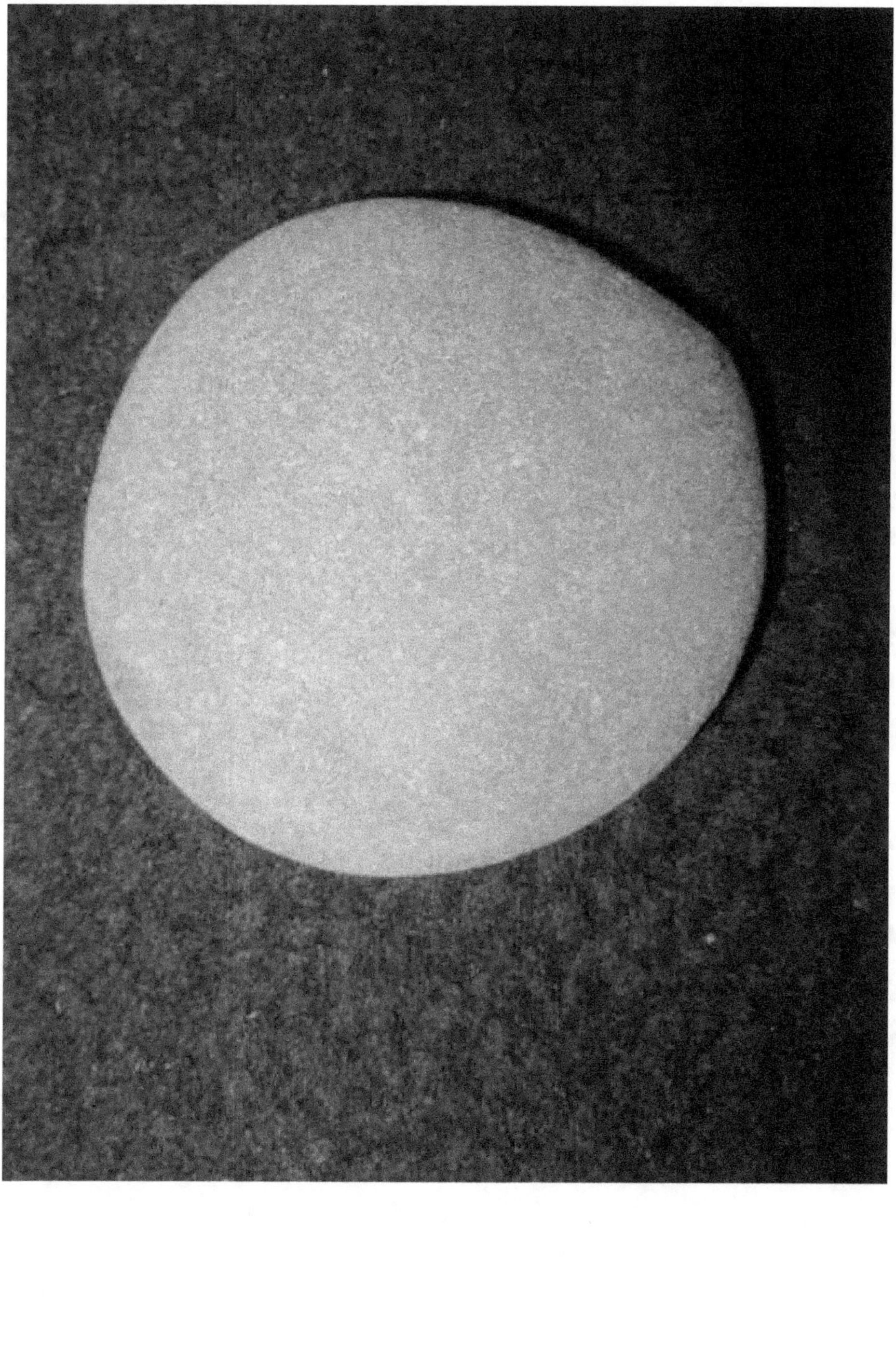

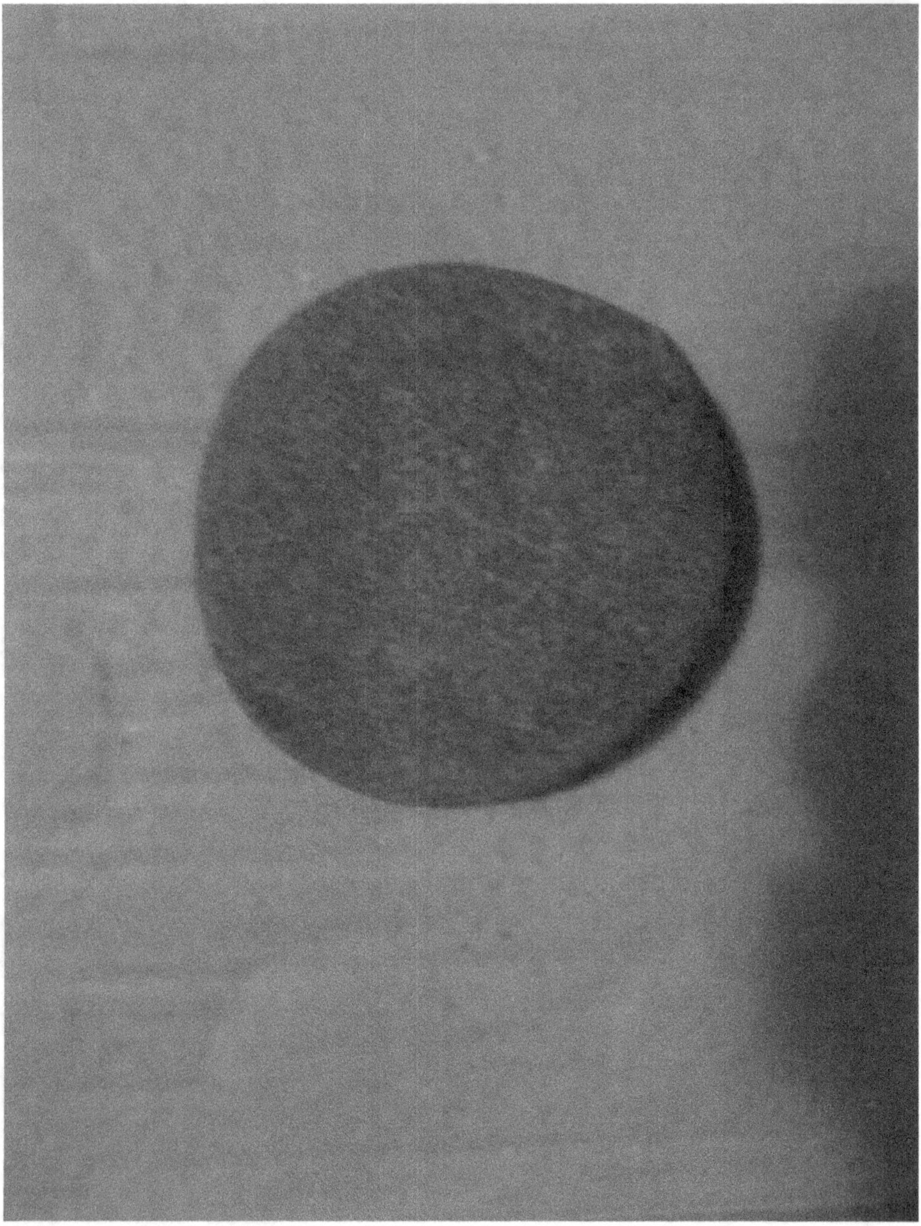

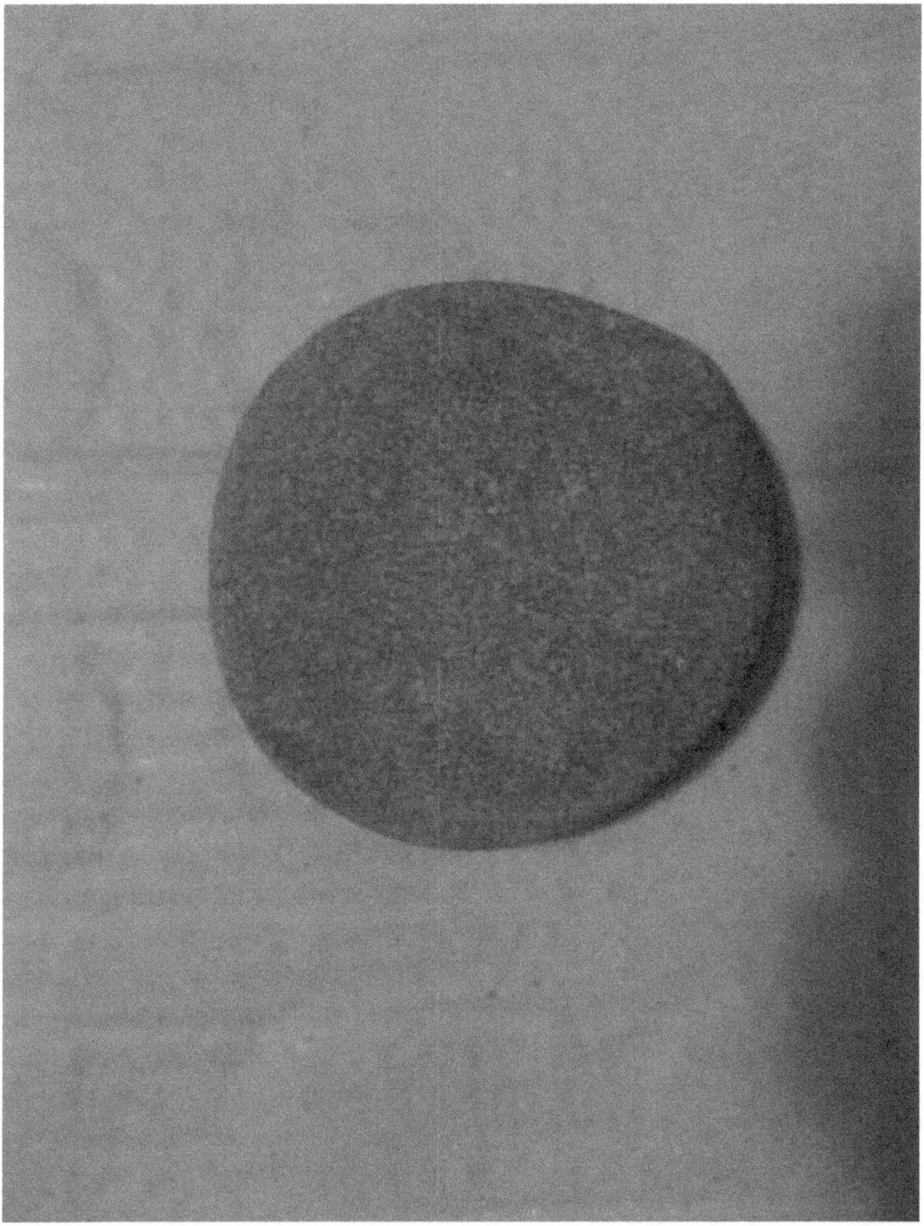

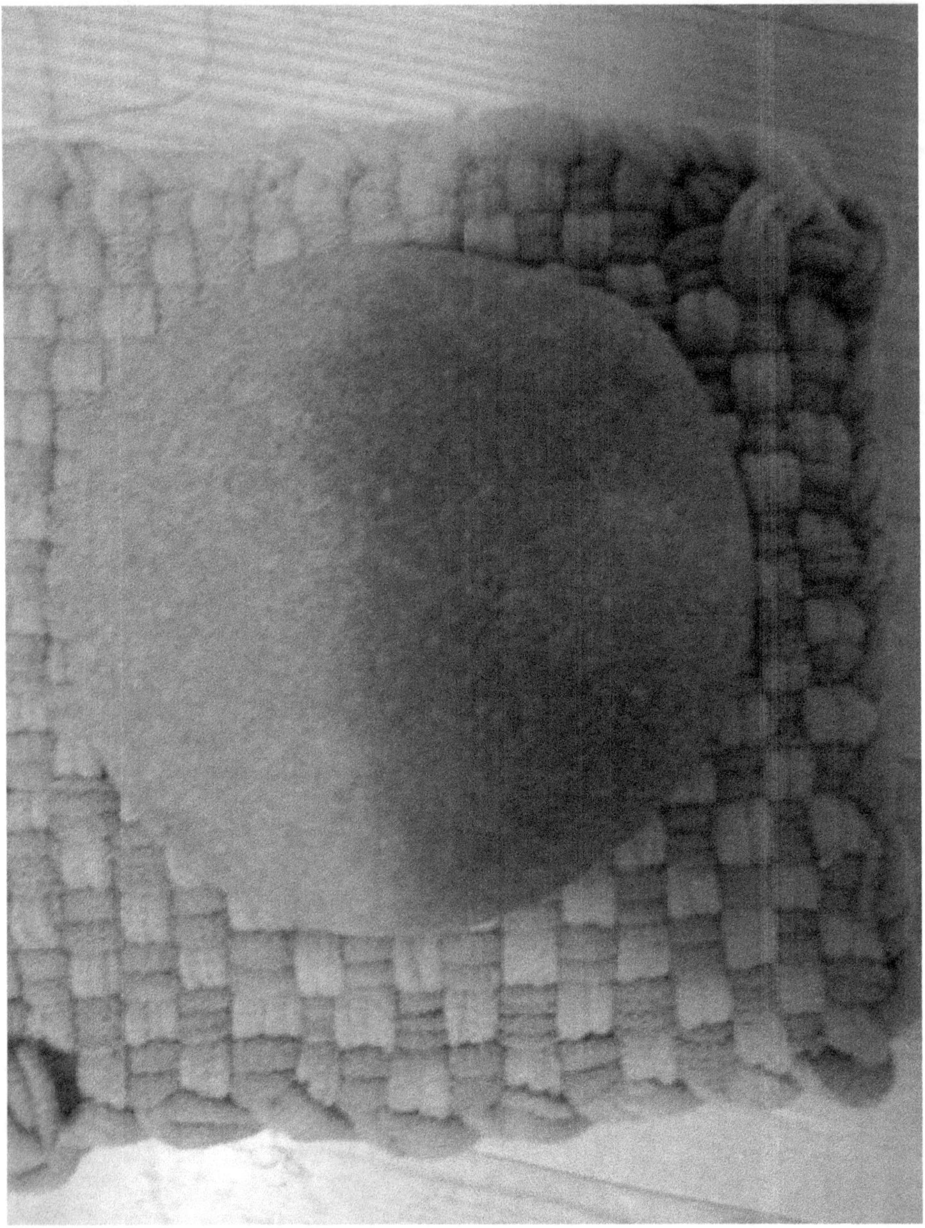

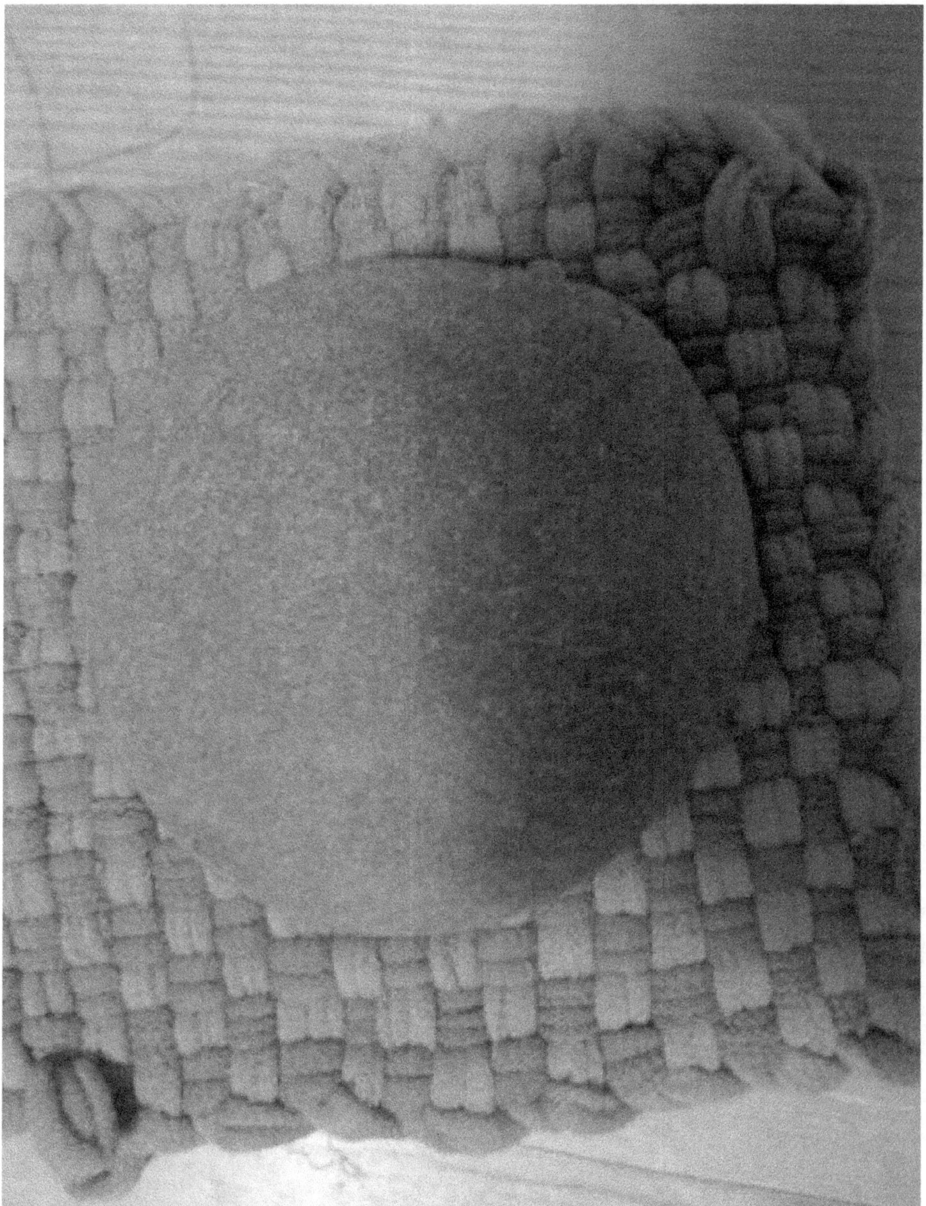

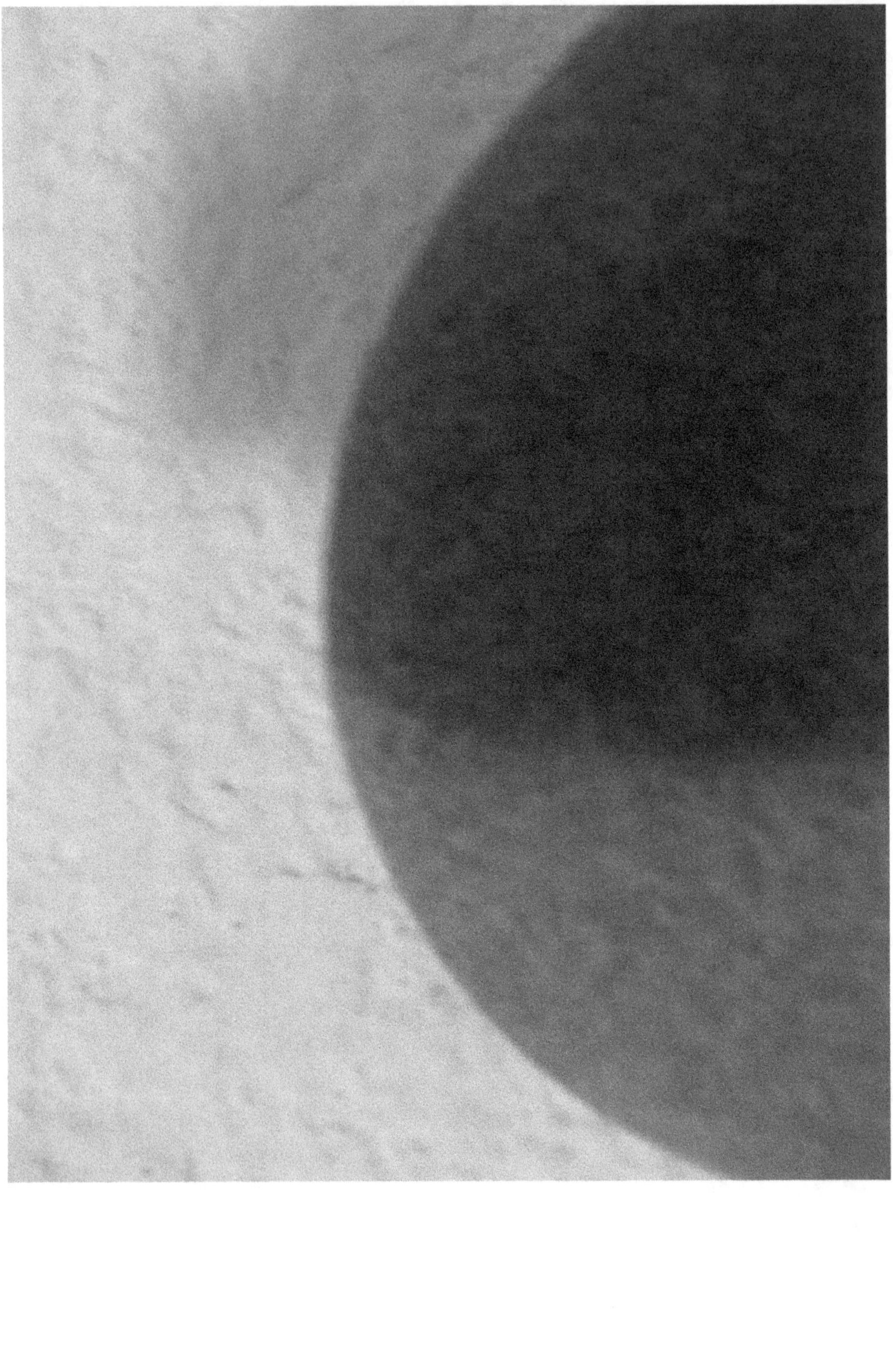

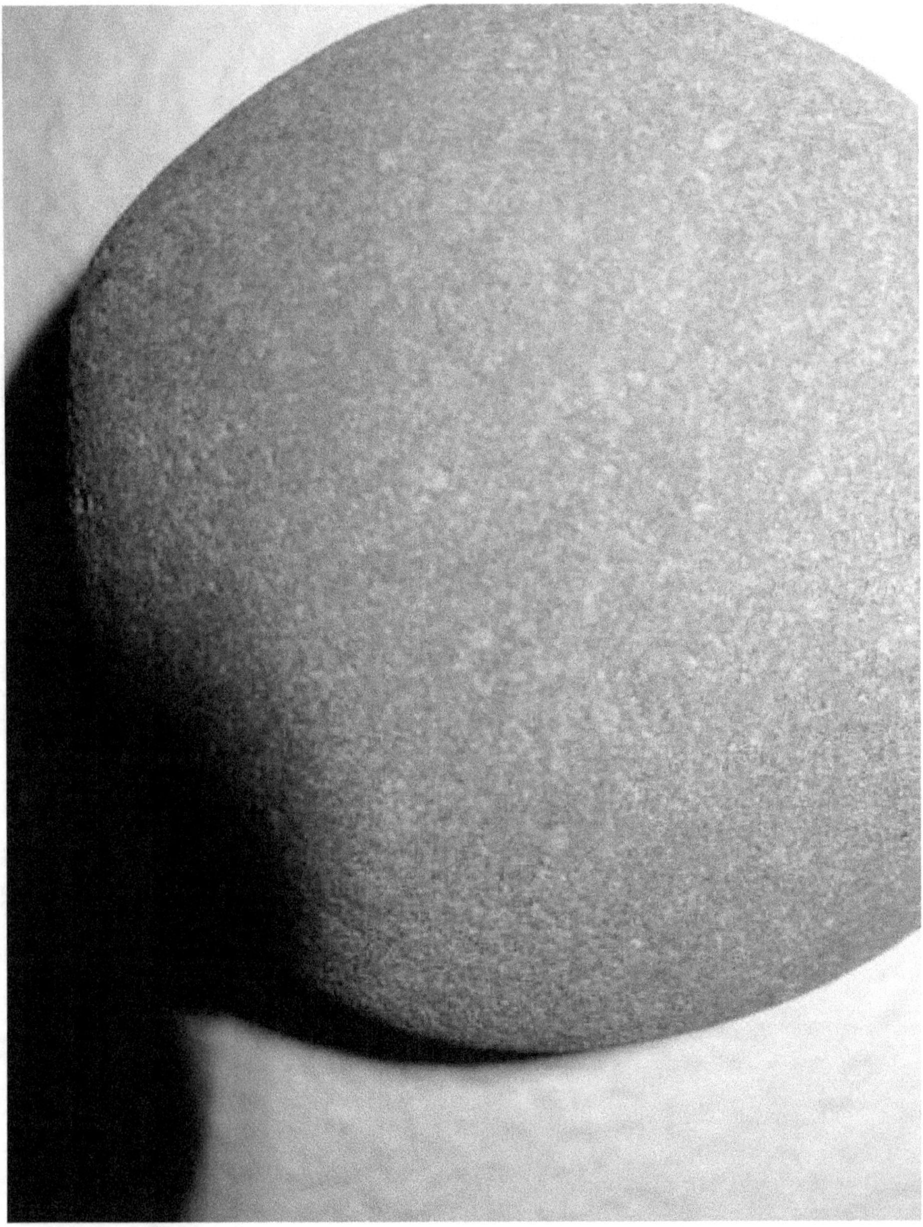

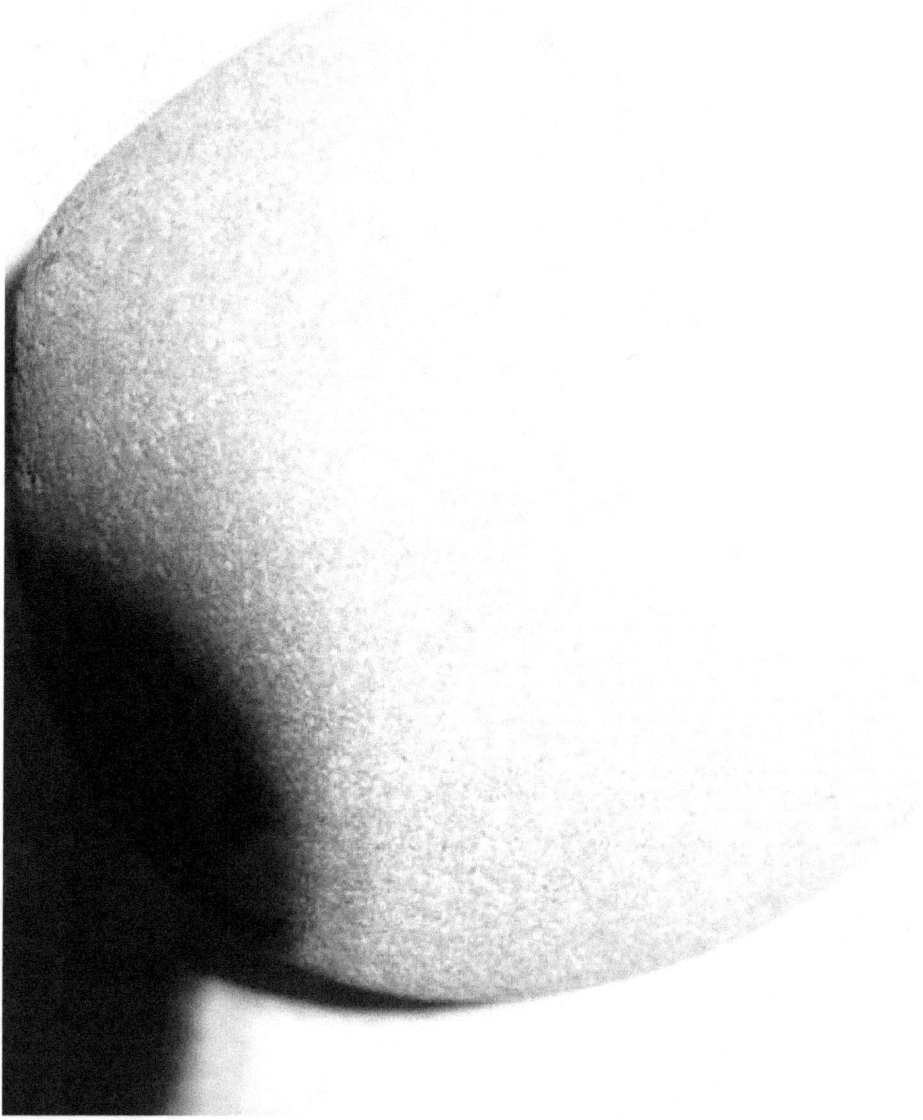

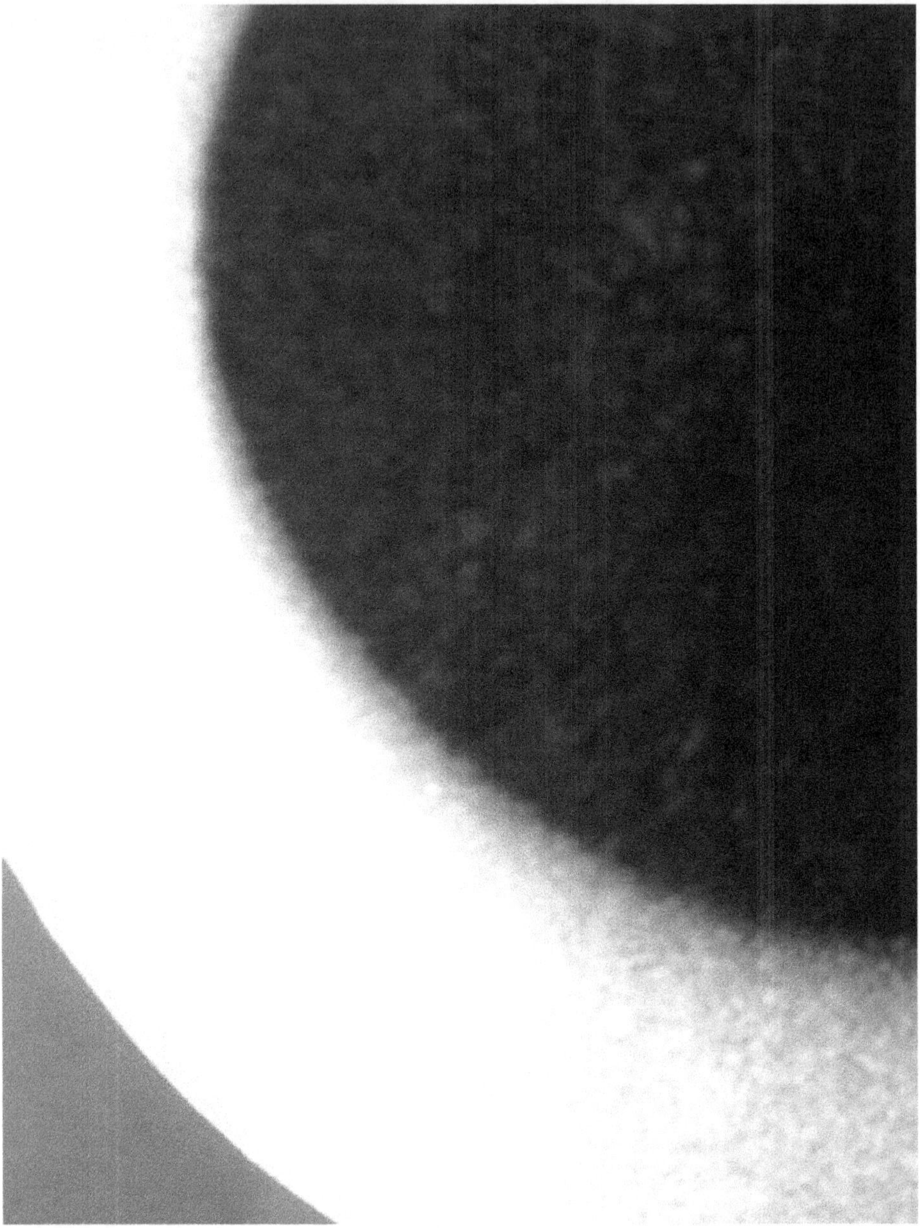

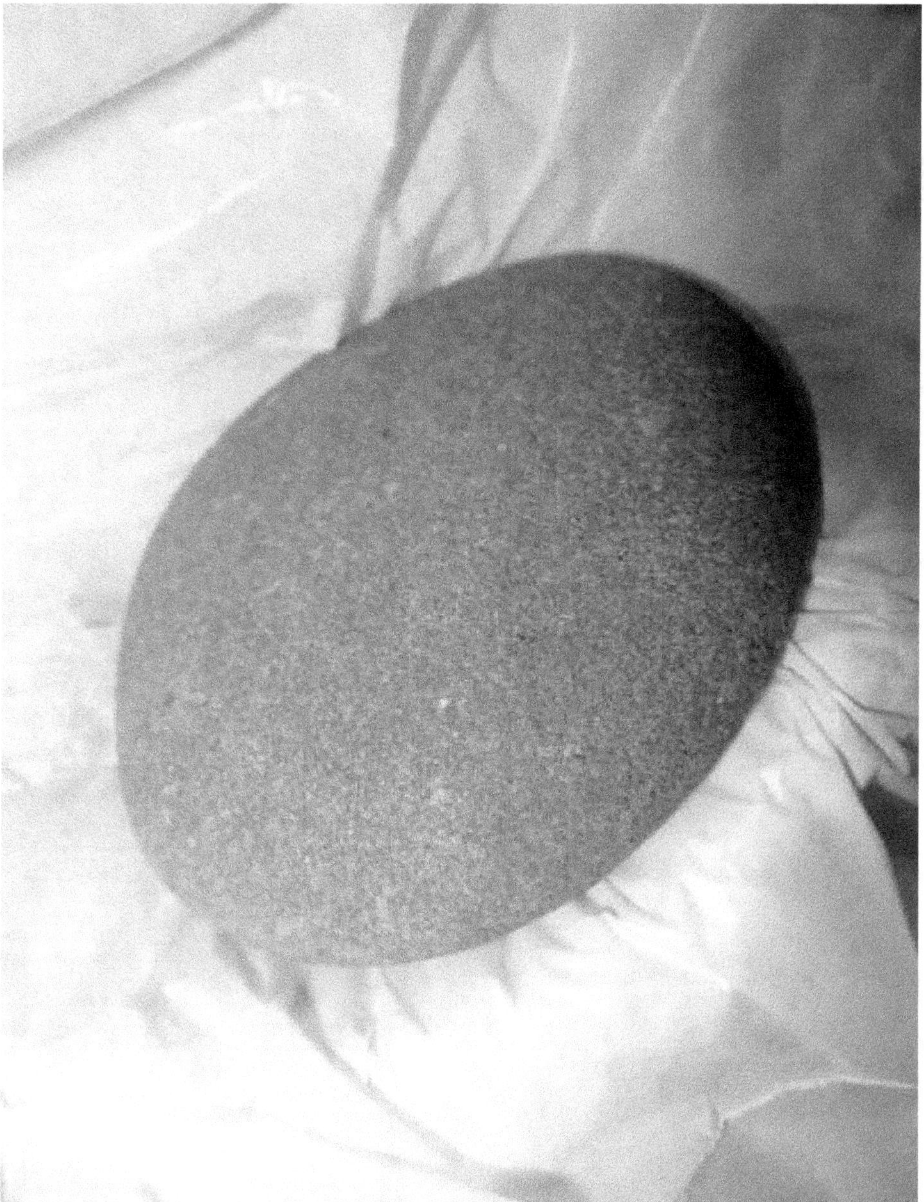

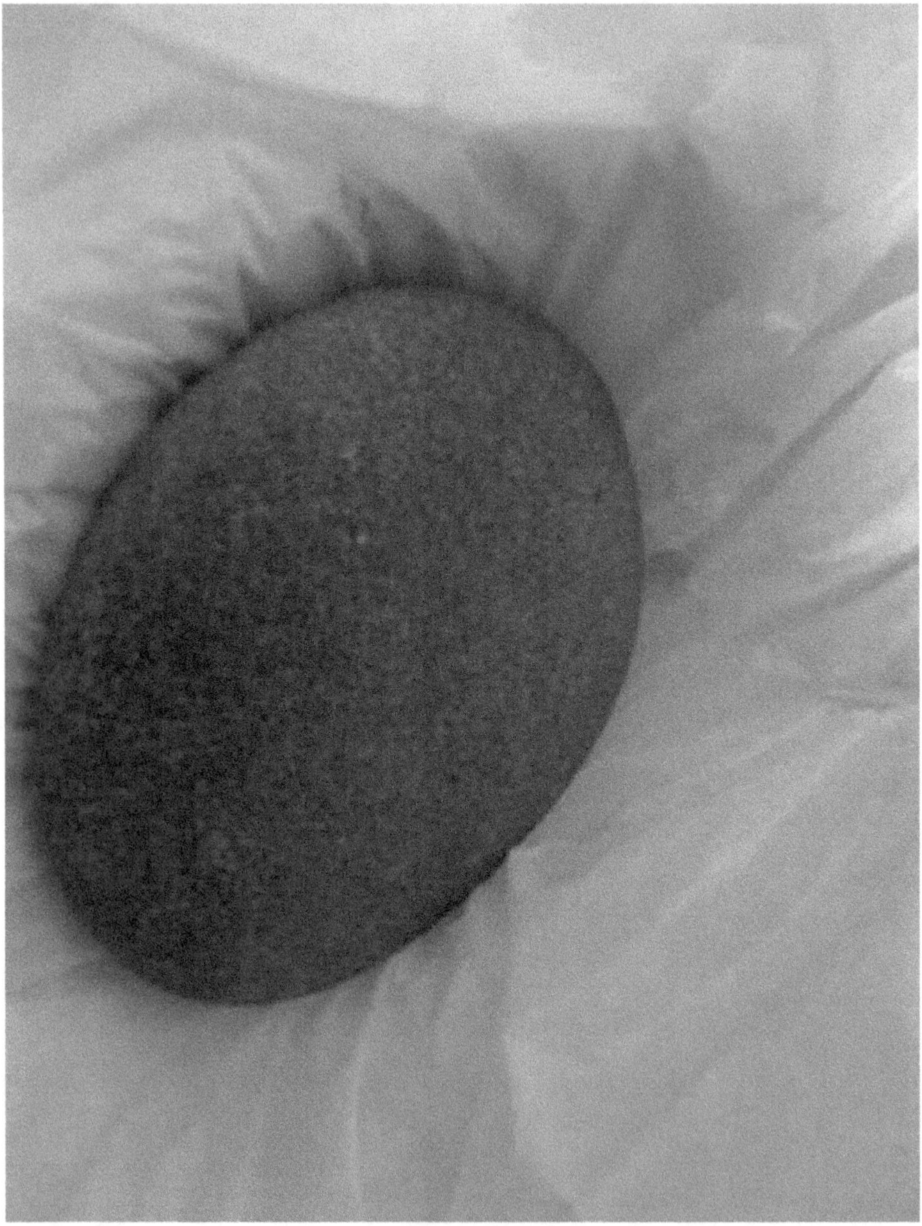

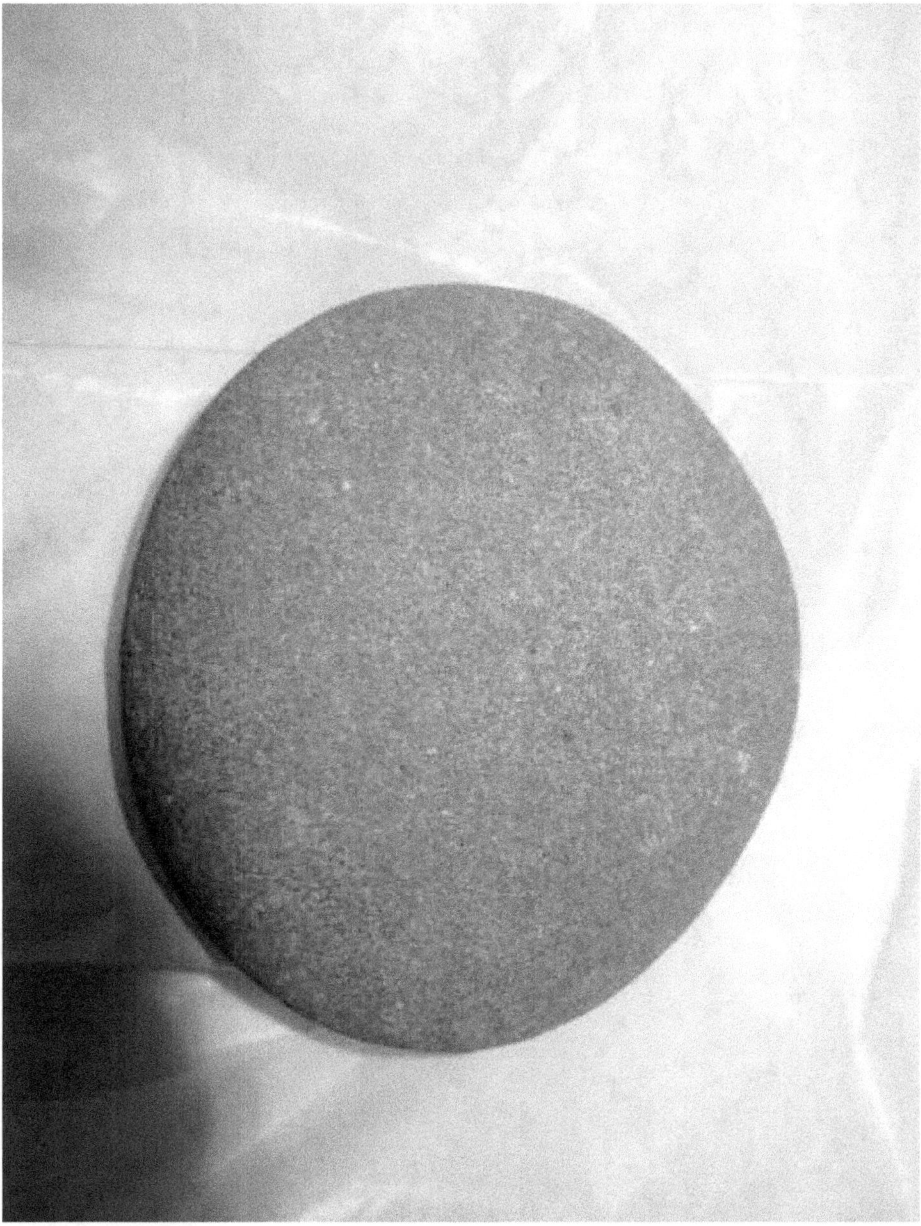

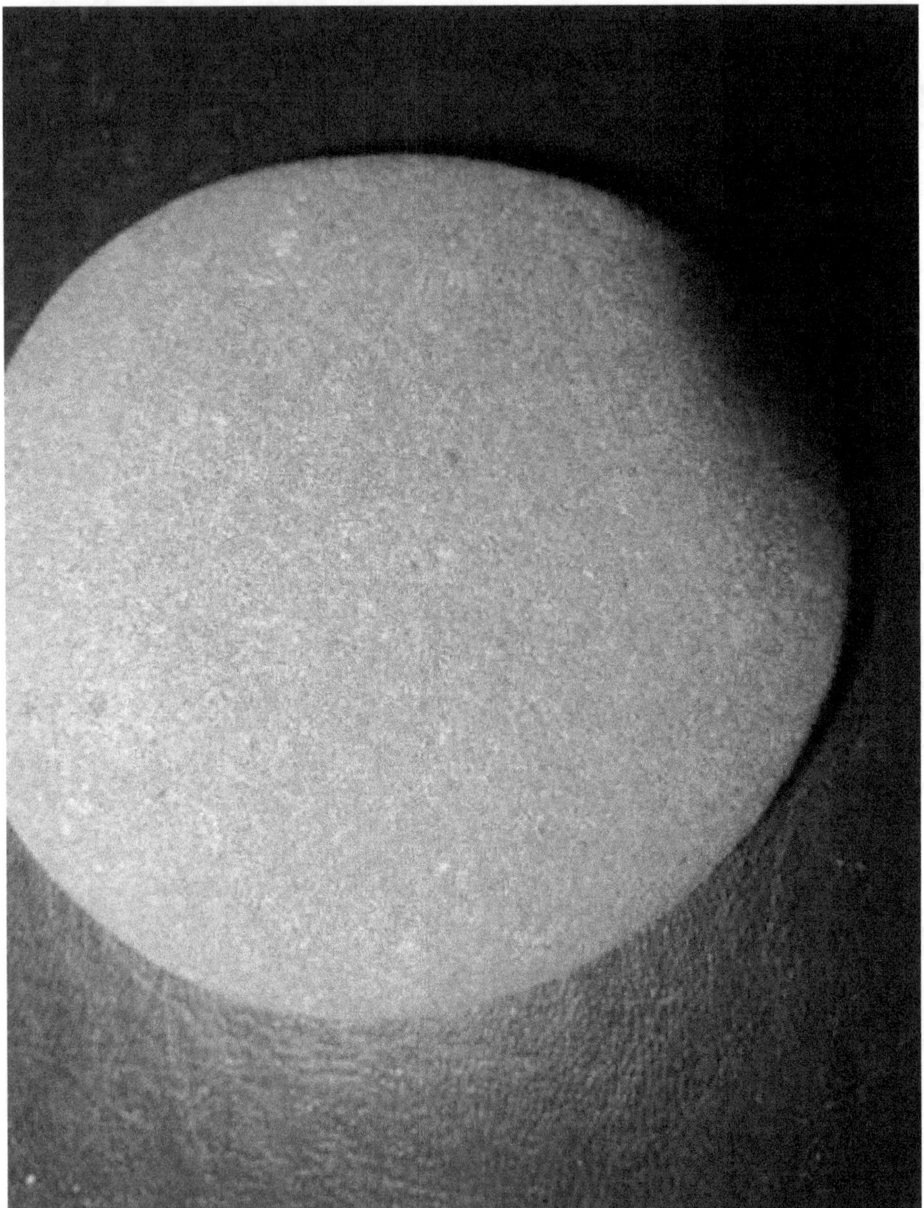

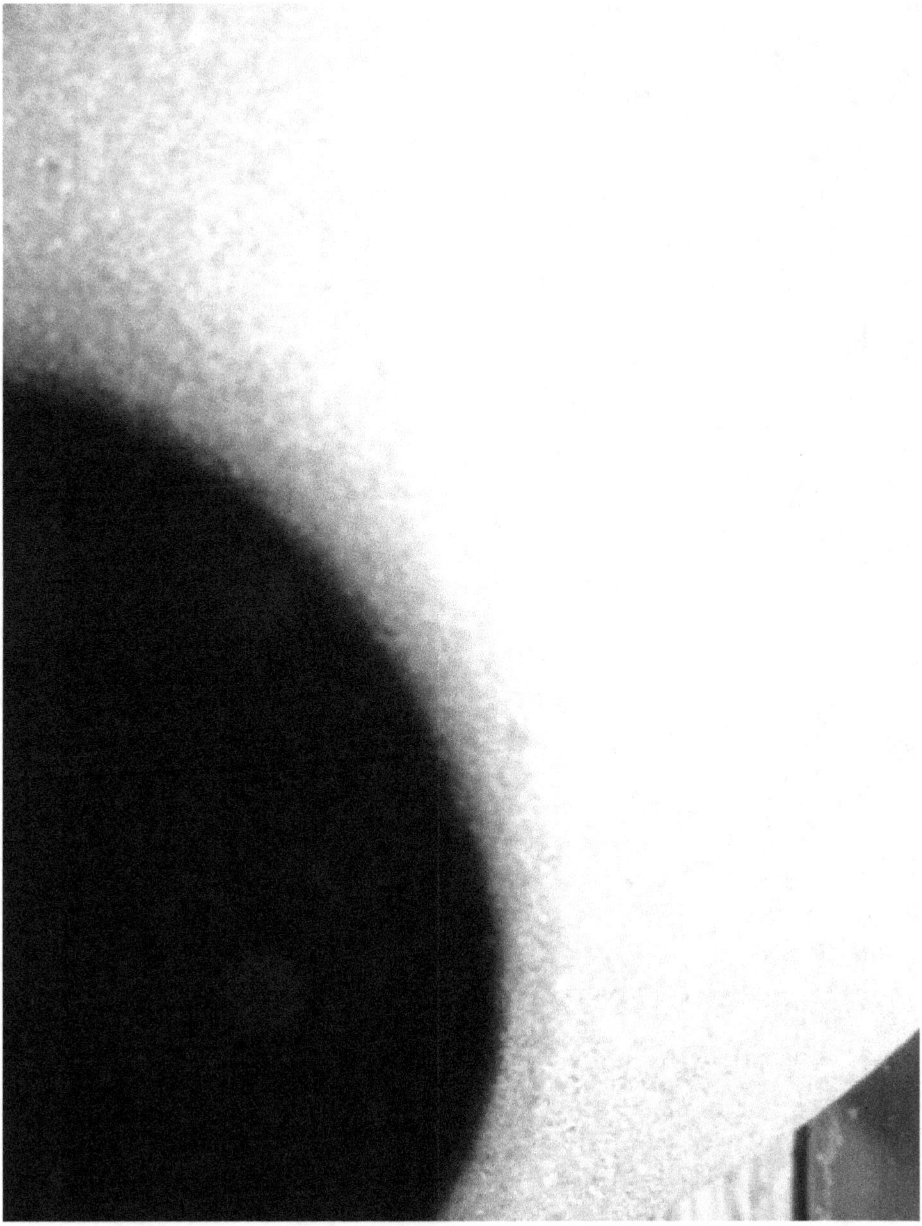

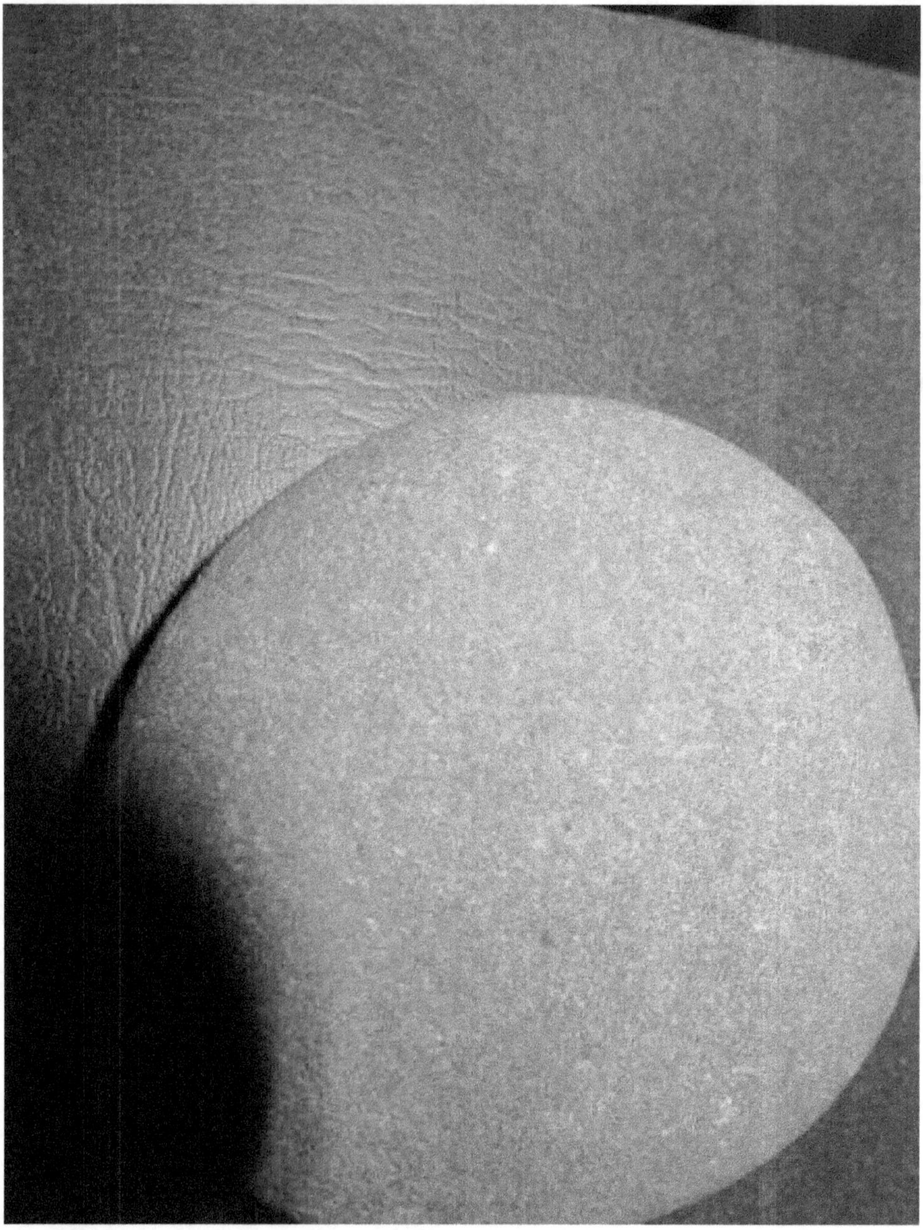

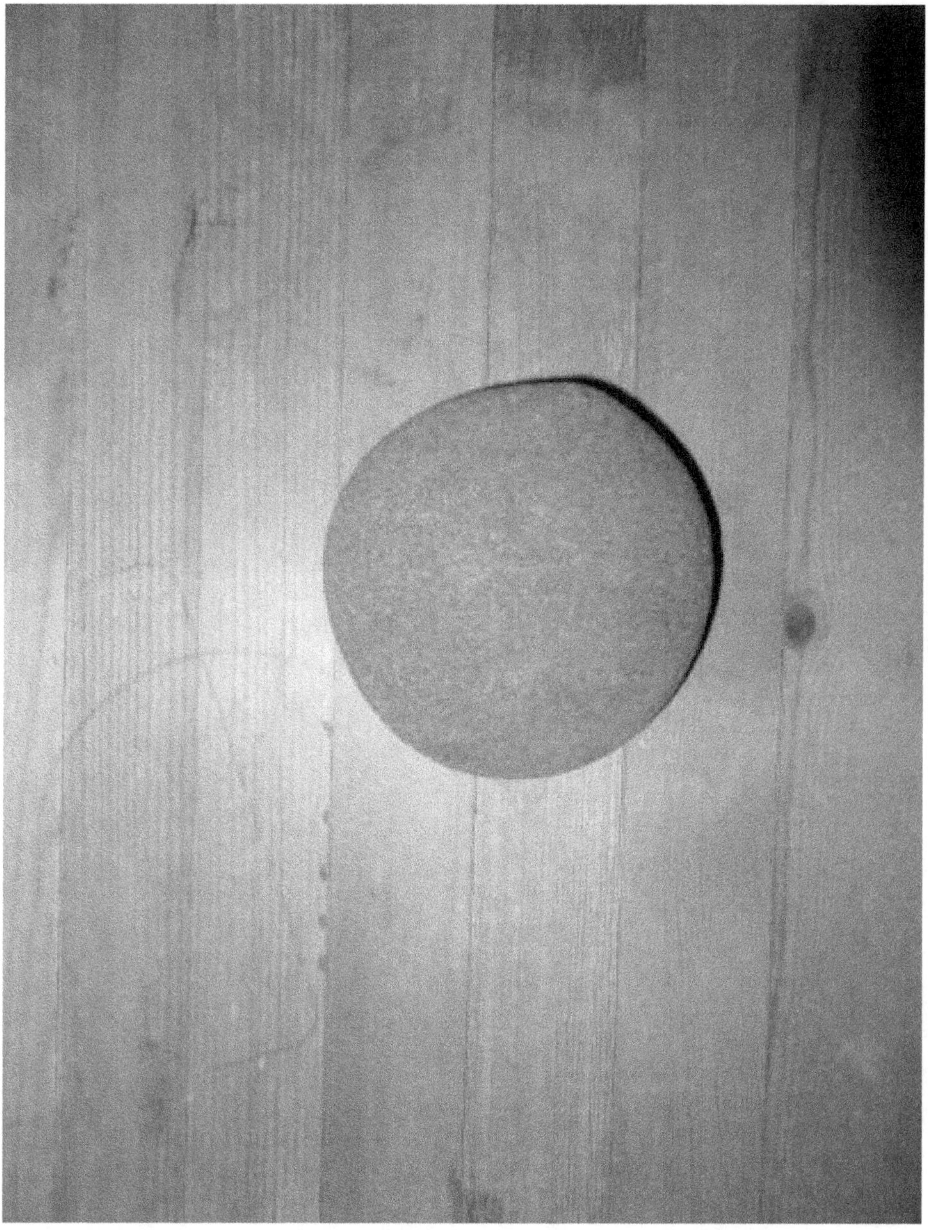

www.ingramcontent.com/pod-product-compliance
Lightning Source LLC
Chambersburg PA
CBHW070730180526
45167CB00004B/1700
* 9 7 8 1 4 9 3 6 9 4 1 5 0 *